Dedicated to 19% of Canadians
who voted for Justin Trudeau.

Thanks a lot.

Journalists all over the world have been swooning over Canada's 23rd Prime Minister Justin Trudeau. They gawk over him, spinning out features and articles on how he's so "dreamy", "charming", "handsome", "sexy" and a "genuine Canadian heartthrob."

What's not to love about Justin?

His illustrious pedigree – born Canadian royalty, the first son of sitting Prime Minister Pierre Elliott Trudeau. His awesome yoga skills. His knowledge of quantum computing. His unabashed embrace of feminism. His tattoos. His love of Syrian refugees. Not to mention that great hair.

Trudeau has become your internet boyfriend. There are endless memes and hot pics of JT, with captions like "Hey Girl, I reserved a spot in my cabinet just for you."

We should all be so lucky.

But the world got to know a different side of Justin Trudeau in late 2016 when he released a bizarre and tone-deaf statement applauding Cuba's socialist dictator, Fidel Castro.

Trudeau unabashedly praised the murderous tyrant, putting his family's friendship with the Castros ahead of common sense and compassion to those who suffered under Castro's heavy-handed dictatorship.

How could Trudeau be that stupid?

Well, for Canadians who pay attention to Trudeau, this is nothing new. Trudeau has always had a habit of putting his foot in his mouth. He has a long history of saying strange and off-putting things that make us feel ashamed and uncomfortable.

The truth about Trudeau is, he isn't very serious. He isn't very thoughtful. He isn't very smart. And, much like a Kim Kardashian or Paris Hilton, Trudeau's status, his wealth and his greatest accomplishments didn't come as a result of merit, hard work or sacrifice, they came from his parents.

Trudeau was born a prince, and, much like his father Pierre, Justin believes that Canada belongs to him.

Those who oppose Trudeau's Leftist agenda cringe at the things he says. We shake our heads and feel embarrassed when he speaks at global conferences and UN meetings. We feel that he doesn't represent our values. He doesn't understand our Canada.

Rather than feel angry, however, we sometimes have to remember to laugh. This book will (hopefully) make you smile, make you laugh, make you shake your head and serve as a gentle reminder of lightness #PMSelfie and all the Stupid Things Trudeau Says.

"I don't read newspapers.
I don't watch the news.
I figure if something important happens, someone will tell me"

# On the Canadian Economy

“A large percentage of small businesses are just ways for wealthier Canadians to save on their taxes”

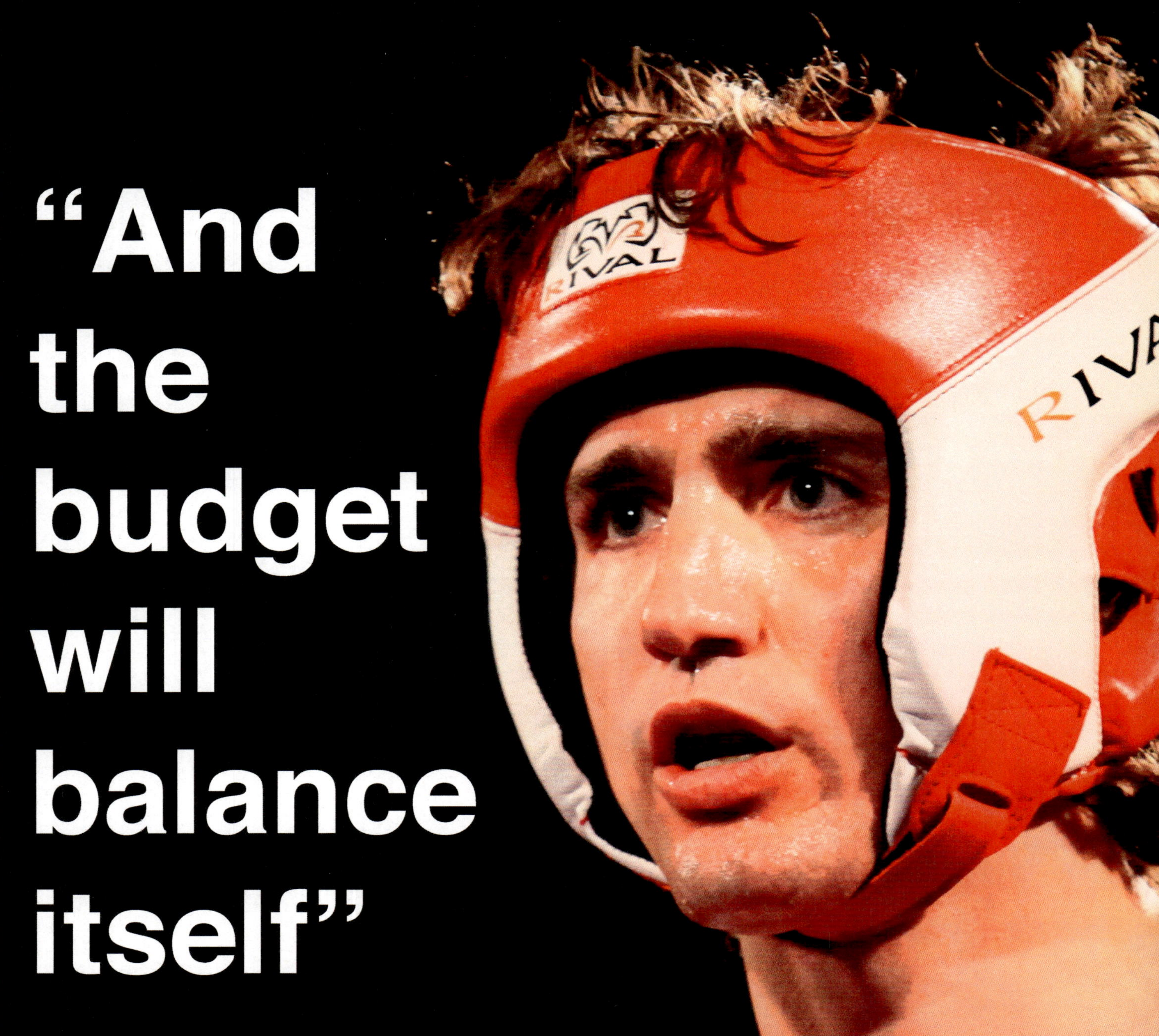
"And
the
budget
will
balance
itself"
RIVAL

"Grow the economy not from the top down like Mr. Harper, but from the heart outwards"

During the 2015 election campaign, Justin Trudeau gave plenty of inspiring speeches.

Trudeau is, after all, a professional speech-giver. He has made a small fortune charging charities and non-profit organizations tens of thousands of dollars in speaker's fees. He's learned how to deliver a barn-burner.

But in his first national election campaign, Trudeau got into trouble when he had to answer questions without speechwriter's notes. His answers had to make some sense. And making sense has never been Trudeau's strong point.

Trudeau proceeded to show a profound lack of understanding when it came to basic economic concepts, like taxes, economic growth and government intervention in the economy.

Maybe for a spoiled trust-fund kid like Justin, small businesses are just a means for tax avoidance, budgets balance themselves and money grows on trees.

But for most Canadians, well, we just shook our heads.

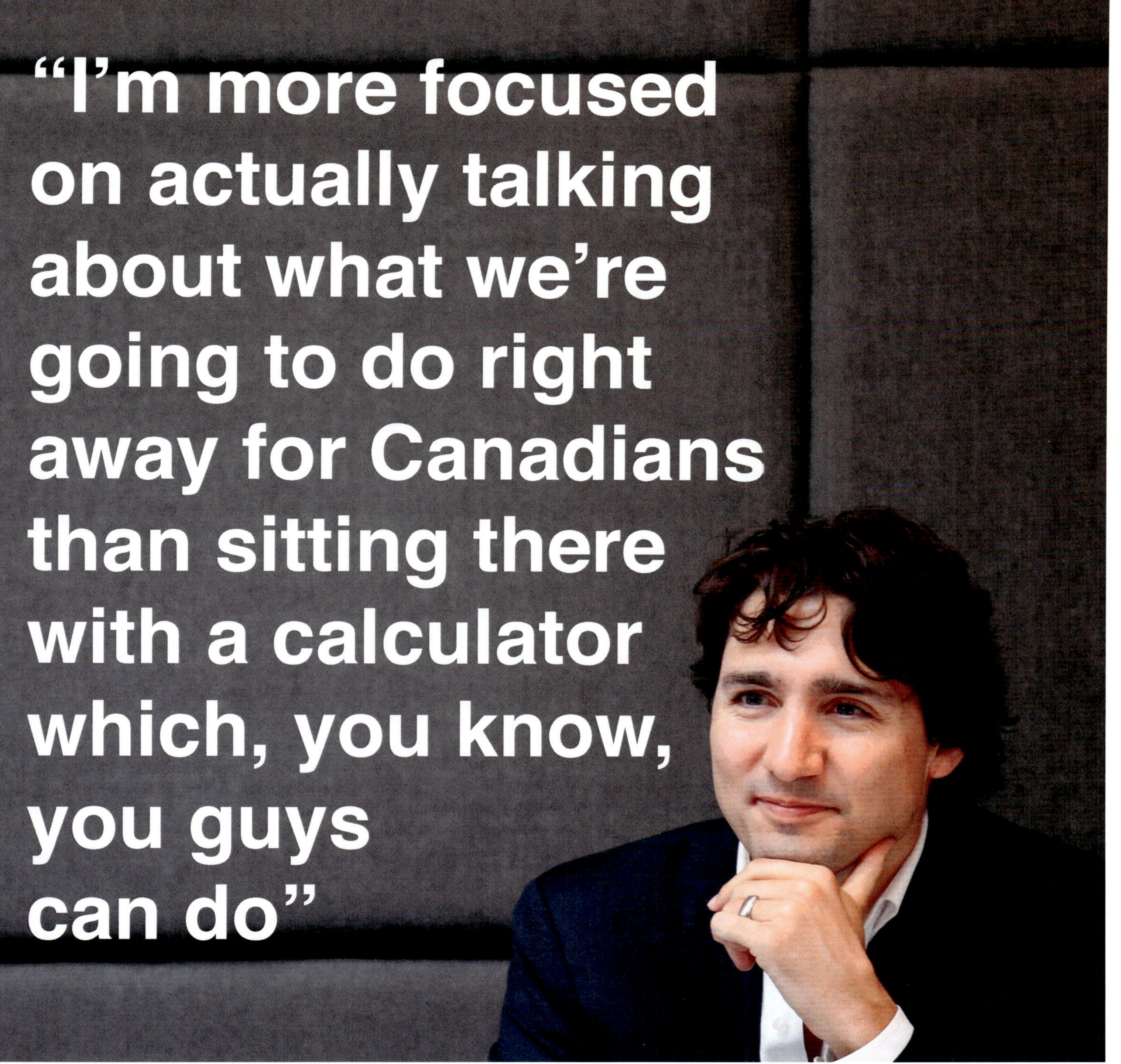
"I'm more focused on actually talking about what we're going to do right away for Canadians than sitting there with a calculator which, you know, you guys can do"

"Deficits are a way of measuring the kind of growth and the kind of success that the government is able to create"
5B

Trudeau shocked the country when he proposed that Canada run “modest deficits” during the 2015 campaign.

Most economists and people who can do math wrote Trudeau off as a neophyte who made a rookie mistake in Canadian federal politics. But some Canadians bought into the idea that the government should borrow cash and dole it out to special interest groups.

Unfortunately for Canadians, after being elected, Trudeau’s “modest deficits” turned into chronic overspending. The 2016 budget deficit was three times higher than Trudeau promised on the campaign trail. The Liberal government will saddle Canadians with more than $130 billion in additional debt by 2022.

Trudeau’s spending spree – bribing us with our money! – is going to leave us in a massive fiscal mess. Trudeau is spending like a drunken sailor and Canadians are going to suffer the hangover.

It’s a heavy price to pay to have a Prime Minister that handsome.

# On Canadian Diplomacy

"What is your favourite Baltic nation?
Uh, that's not a thing"
FINLAND
NORWAY
SWEDEN
DENMARK
ESTONIA
LATVIA
LITHUANIA
POLAND
GERMANY
BELARUS
RUSSIA
Gulf of Bothnia
Gulf of Finland
Gulf of Riga
Baltic Sea
Skagerrak
Kattegat
Trondheim
Vaasa
Sundsvall
Oslo
Stavanger
Stockholm
Turku
Helsinki
St. Petersburg
Tallinn
Riga
Vilnius
Minsk
Copenhagen
Malmö
Kiel
Gdansk
Kaliningrad (RUSSIA)
Luleå
Oulu
NORTH
Kilometres

**“It is with deep sorrow that I learned today of the death of Cuba’s longest serving President.**

**Fidel Castro was a larger than life leader who served his people for almost half a century. A legendary revolutionary and orator, Mr. Castro made significant improvements to the education and healthcare of his island nation.**

While a controversial figure, both Mr. Castro's supporters and detractors recognized his tremendous dedication and love for the Cuban people who had a deep and lasting affection for "el Commandant

I know my father was very proud to call him a friend and I had the opportunity to meet Fidel when my father passed away. It was also a real honour to meet his three sons and his brother President Raúl Castro during my recent visit to Cuba.

On behalf of all Canadians, Sophie and I offer our deepest condolences to the family, friends and many, many supporters of Mr. Castro. We join the people of Cuba today in mourning the loss of this remarkable leader."

“It's very worrying, especially because Russia lost in hockey, they'll be in a bad mood”

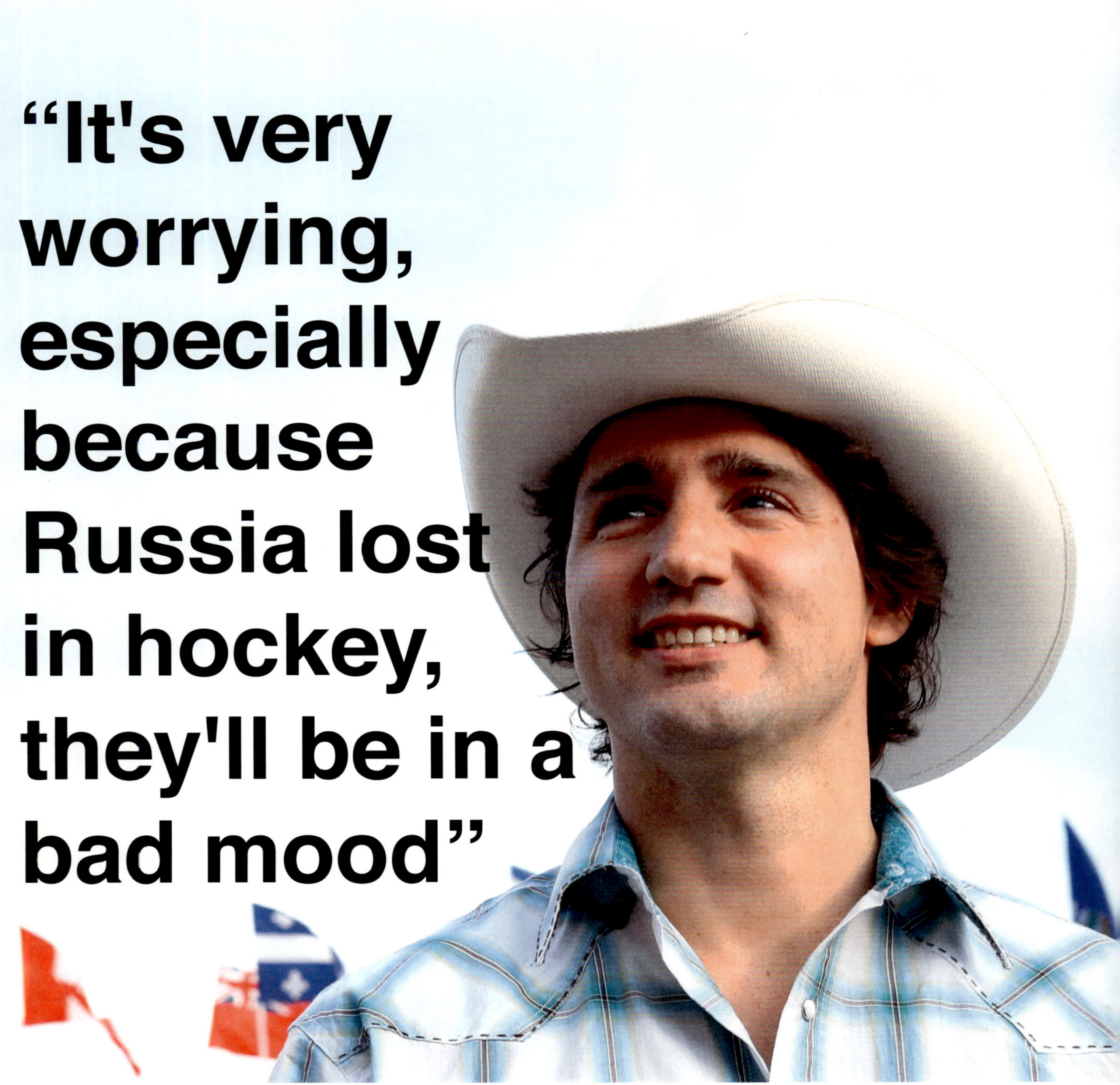

Former PM Stephen Harper famously stood up to belligerent Russian President Vladimir Putin. During a G20 summit, Putin tried to shake Harper's hand. Harper responded,

"I guess I'll shake your hand." He then firmly said, "But I only have one thing to say to you. Get out of Ukraine."

Harper did what every other world leader was afraid to do.

While Barack Obama, David Cameron and Angela Merkel all cowered to Putin's invasion of a sovereign state, Harper stepped in and stood up to the Russian bully.

During the foreign policy debate in the 2015 election campaign, the moderator asked Trudeau if he, too, would stand up to Putin.

The audience burst into laughter.

Even downtown Toronto elites couldn't imagine Trudeau having the spine to stand up to bullies. Trudeau is more of a mascot. He makes us feel warm and fuzzy, happy and hopeful.

Bring up anything serious, though, and Trudeau will revert back to being a class clown who makes silly jokes about the complex issues he just doesn't understand.

"There is a level of admiration I actually have for China. Because of their, you know, basic dictatorship is allowing them to actually turn their economy around on a dime"

**"Having a little more of an awareness of what's going on in the rest of the world I think is what many Canadians would hope for Americans"**

**Reporter:**
**“Would a Liberal government prioritize ethnic and religious minorities?”**

**Trudeau:**
**“Absolutely not”**

“Somewhere in the Prime Minister’s Office, staffers were pouring through their personal files, to try to find out which families would be suitable for a photo op for the Prime Minister’s re-election campaign. That’s disgusting”

# On the War against Terrorism

“The Liberal Party
believes that terrorists
should get to keep
their Canadian
citizenship.
Because I do”

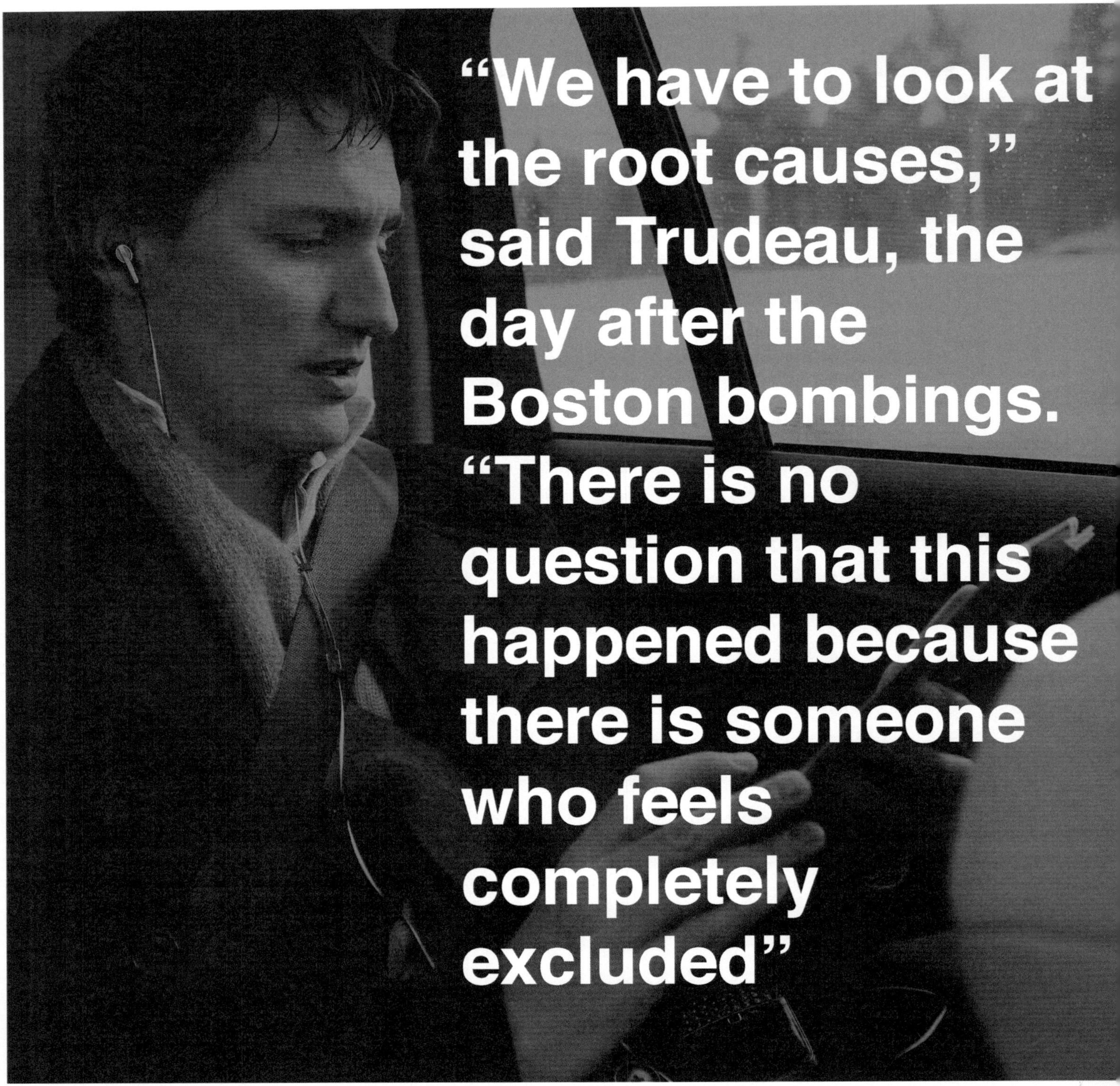

"We have to look at the root causes," said Trudeau, the day after the Boston bombings. "There is no question that this happened because there is someone who feels completely excluded"

In the wake of a deadly terrorist attack during the Boston Marathon, which we later learned was perpetrated by Islamist refugees with allegiance to a terrorist organization, Trudeau felt the need to lecture Canadians and tell us to think about the "root causes" of terrorism.

These ruthless killers, according to Trudeau, were probably just victims of social exclusion.

During the CBC interview, Trudeau didn't mention those killed or maimed, their families or the immense suffering the terrorists needlessly inflicted upon innocent civilians. He didn't mention the threat free societies face by fanatical religious zealots who believe in martyrdom and jihad against infidels.

Instead, Trudeau delved into a rambling, incoherent rant about tolerance and trying to understand terrorists.

When it came to responding to the Boston terrorist attacks, Trudeau did not sound like a future Prime Minister.

He sounded like a high school student. And not a particularly smart one.

**"There are things that Canada can do that other countries wouldn't be able to do… there are a lot of people, refugees and displaced persons, fleeing violence facing a very very cold winter in the mountains. That's something Canada has expertise on: how to face a winter in the mountains"**

**“Rather than trying to whip out our CF18’s to show them how big they are.”**

# On Being a Feminist

"Because it's 2015"
Happy
New
Year

Trudeau loves to remind us that he is a feminist. It may be his favourite thing about himself.

When it came to appointing his cabinet —the inner circle that runs key functions of the government —Trudeau went out of his way to ensure that women held half the positions.

Unfortunately for Canada, that included promoting many young, inexperienced and highly unqualified women to top government positions.

Rather than selecting the best person for the job, Trudeau's affirmative action appointments separated the cabinet into two categories, men and women, and women only had to compete with the other women for a cabinet position.

Hiring an unqualified woman over a qualified man is not feminism. It's sexism. And it's offensive to women.

Trudeau is virtue singling, and his silly answer to the question of why he appointed a "gender-neutral" cabinet ("because it's 2015"), shows that he sees women as just another special interest group to appease through big government.

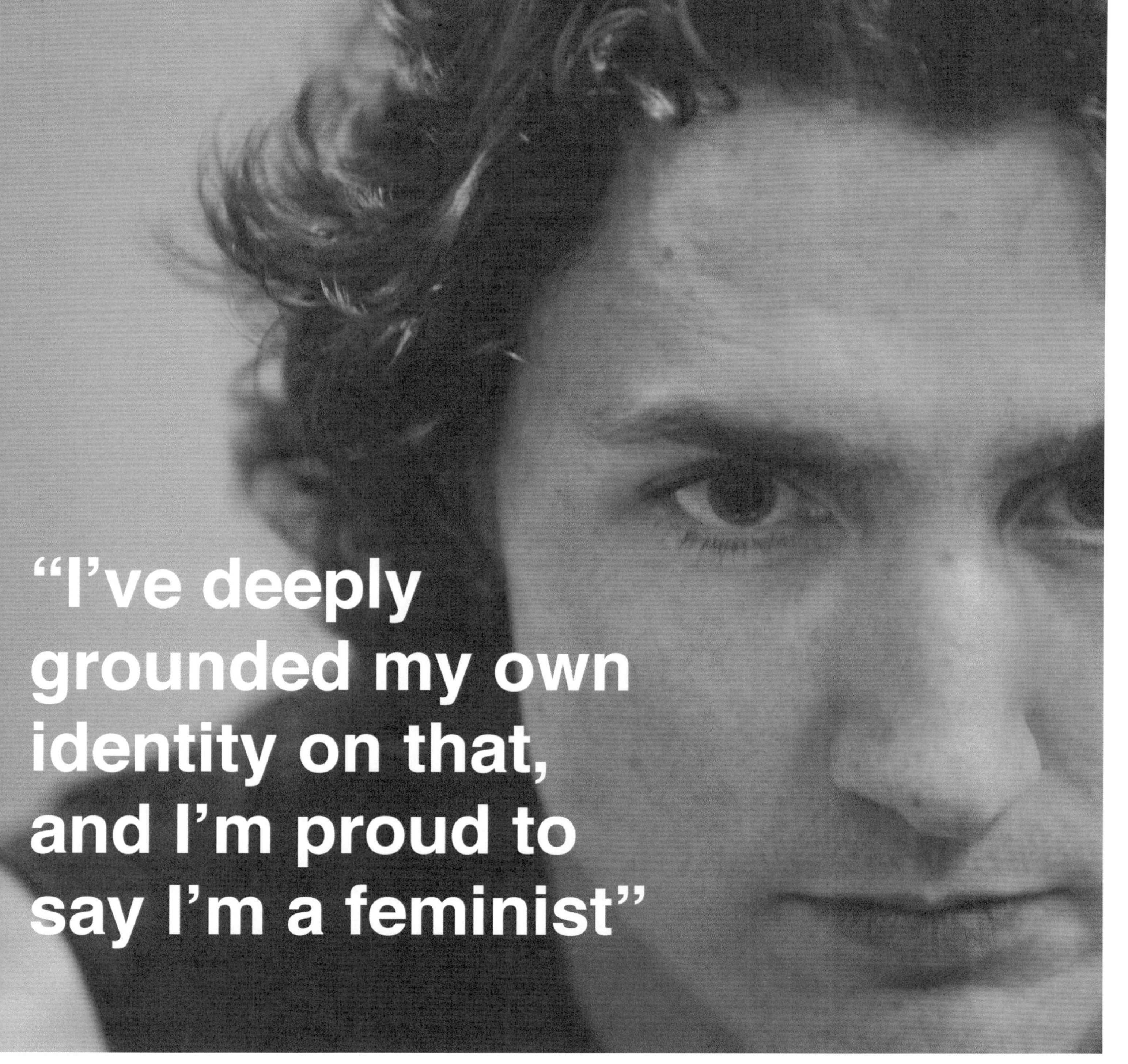
"I've deeply
grounded my own
identity on that,
and I'm proud to
say I'm a feminist"

“Quite frankly I talk about the fact that I’m a feminist as often as I can”

"I'll just keep saying I'm a feminist until there is no reaction"

# Barbaric Cultural Practices? Trudeau says using the term "barbaric" to describe female genital mutilation and honour killings is "too harsh"

**“We are a place that has figured out that diversity can be a source of strength… as I look at this beautiful room, with the sisters upstairs.” Trudeau said, at a segregated mosque where women are banned from the main floor.**

# On Canadian Identity

"There is no
core identity,
no mainstream
in Canada"

While speaking to an American journalist at the New York Times magazine, Justin Trudeau told us what he really thinks.

He said he believed that Canada is not defined by "its European history" but by a "pan-cultural heritage." He wants us to become a "post-national state."

But Canada didn't just happen. We are not simply a hodgepodge of different people from different places with different values who just happen to live side-by-side.

Canada is not a random movie theatre full of strangers on opening night of the latest Star Wars movie. Canada is a nation. And we have a lot to be proud of.

Our culture and values are deeply rooted in our Western heritage and traditions. We are part of the legacy of the greatest civilization in human history.

And while you certainly don't need to be of European ancestry to be a Canadian, you cannot deny that our free, peaceful, law-abiding and prosperous society is built upon on the ideals and the traditions of our British & French political forefathers.

That Trudeau can't see that, is stunning, even for Trudeau.

Canada is
“the first
post-national
state”

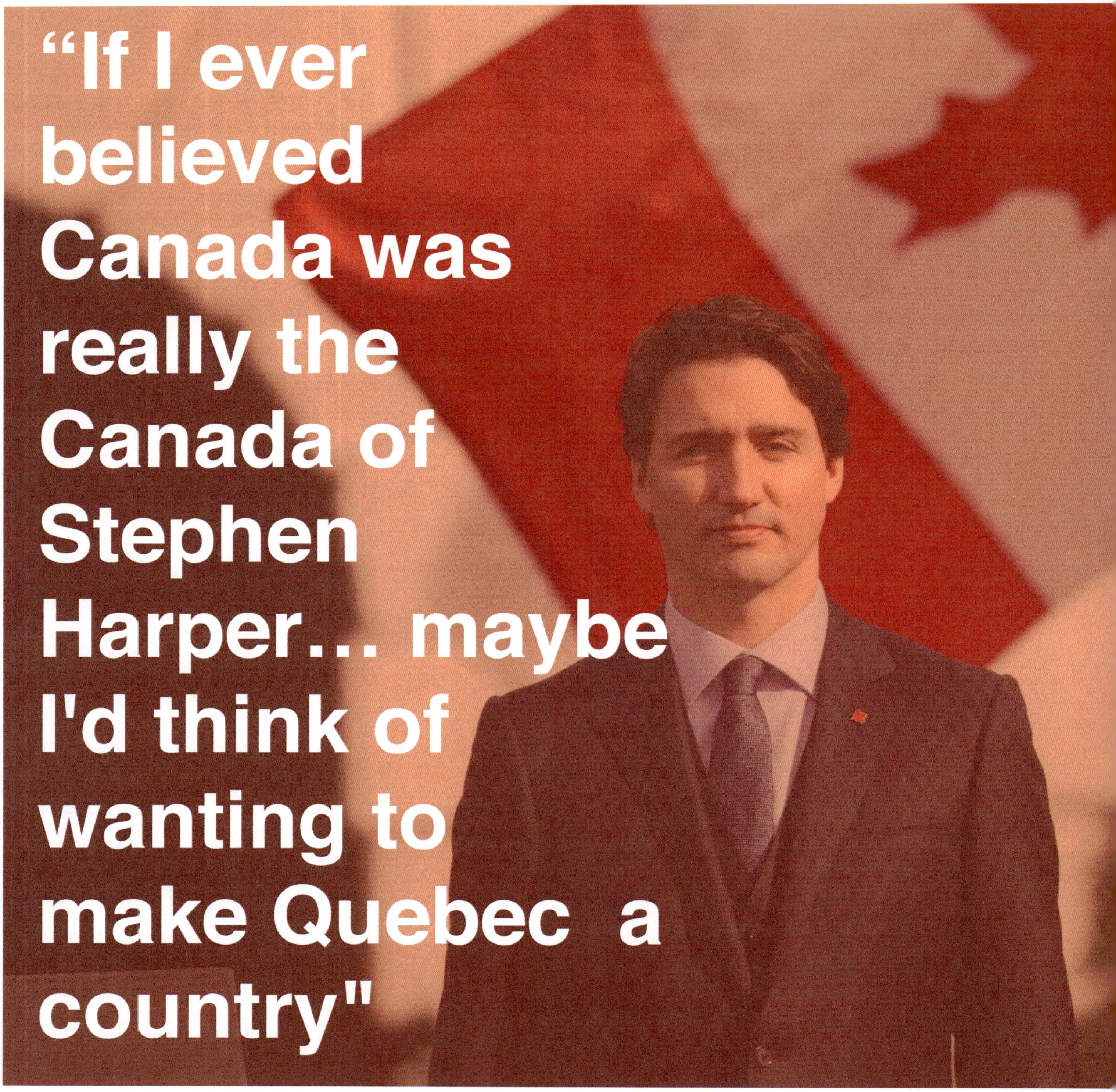

“If I ever believed Canada was really the Canada of Stephen Harper… maybe I'd think of wanting to make Quebec  a country"

During a celebrity appearance on US television, Justin Trudeau wore a shirt that said “Global Citizen” — the name of an international charity.

Given Trudeau’s aspirations to remake Canada into a “post-national state,” and given his preference to pour billions of Canadian dollars into foreign projects, it’s fair to ask:

Does Trudeau consider himself first a citizen of Canada, or a citizen of the world?

Citizenship means membership in a community. It implies loyalty, patriotism and duty. Does Trudeau side with hardworking Canadians or with UN bureaucrats?

While Trudeau doesn’t seem to have a very high opinion of Canadians, particularly hardworking folks in Western Canada, he does have an affinity for Quebec separatists.

Prior to becoming Prime Minister, Trudeau regularly made anti-Canadian, pro-separatist remarks.

Can you imagine any other politician so eager to divide Canadians and pit different groups against each other?

Oh Justin. You’re lucky you’re so handsome.

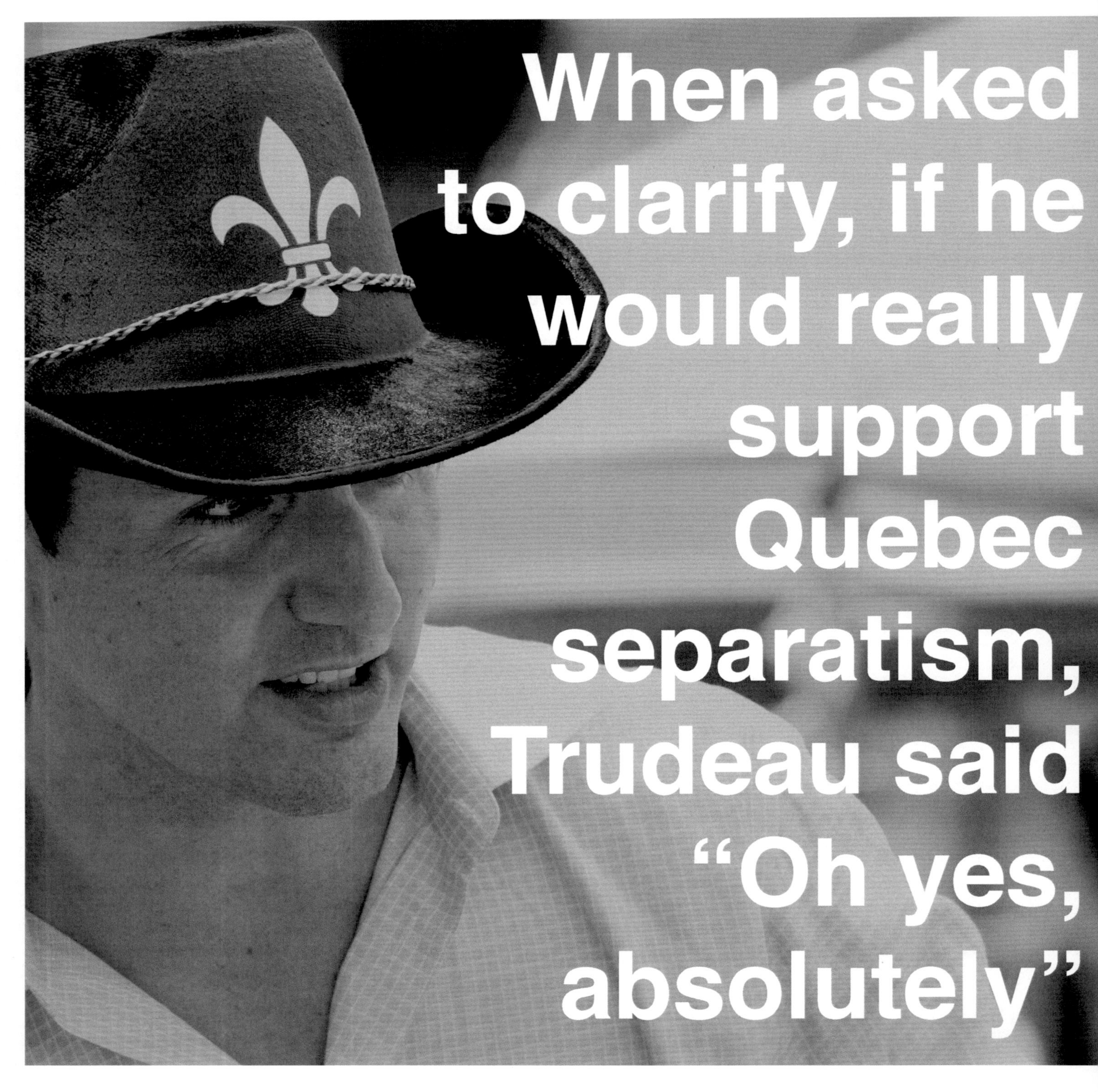
When asked to clarify, if he would really support Quebec separatism, Trudeau said “Oh yes, absolutely”

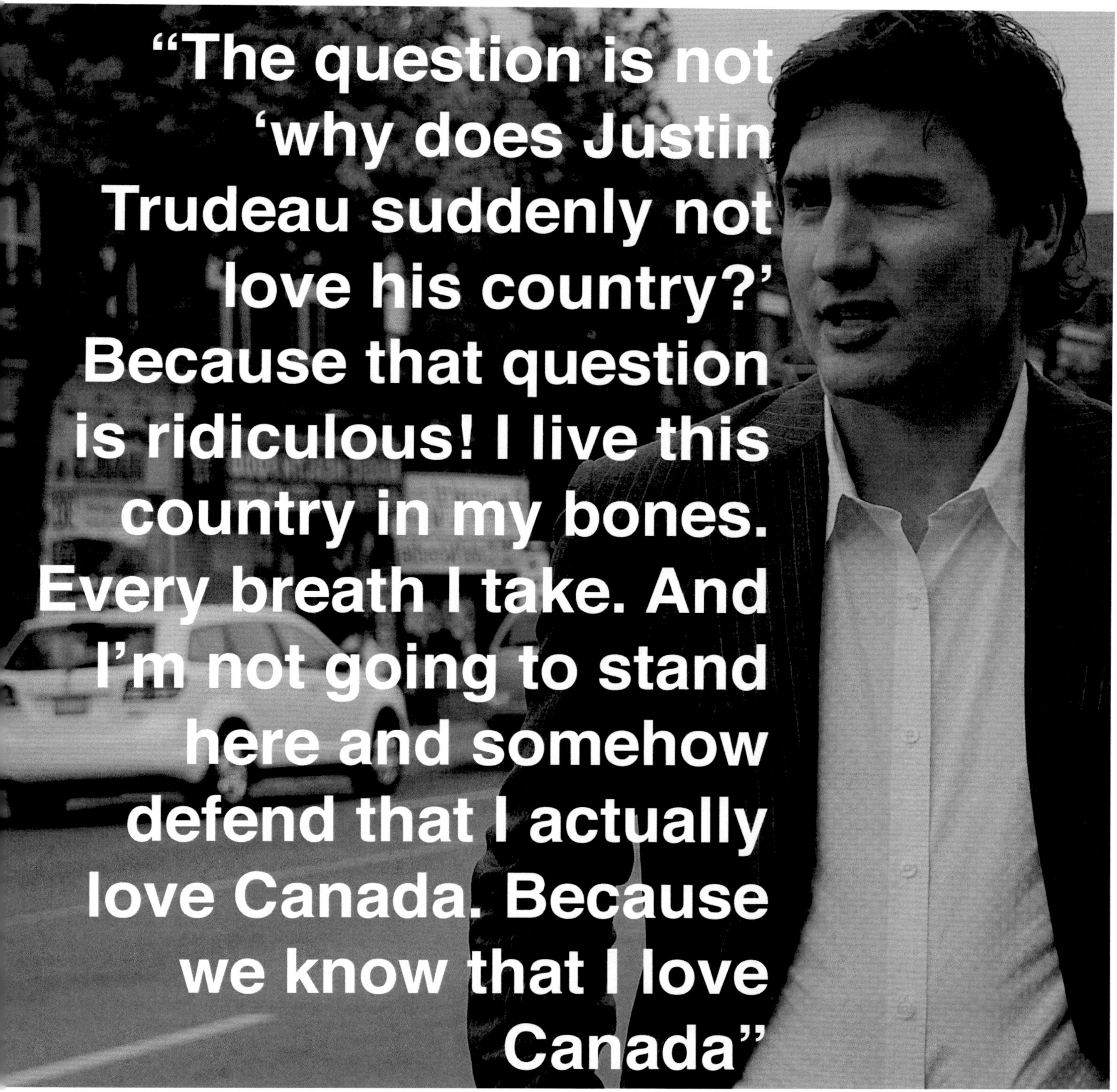

“The question is not ‘why does Justin Trudeau suddenly not love his country?’ Because that question is ridiculous! I live this country in my bones. Every breath I take. And I’m not going to stand here and somehow defend that I actually love Canada. Because we know that I love Canada”

# On Quebec Supremacy

“Quebecers are better than the rest of Canada, because, you know, we’re Quebecers”

"Canada isn't doing well right now because it's Albertan's who control our collective socio-democratic agenda"

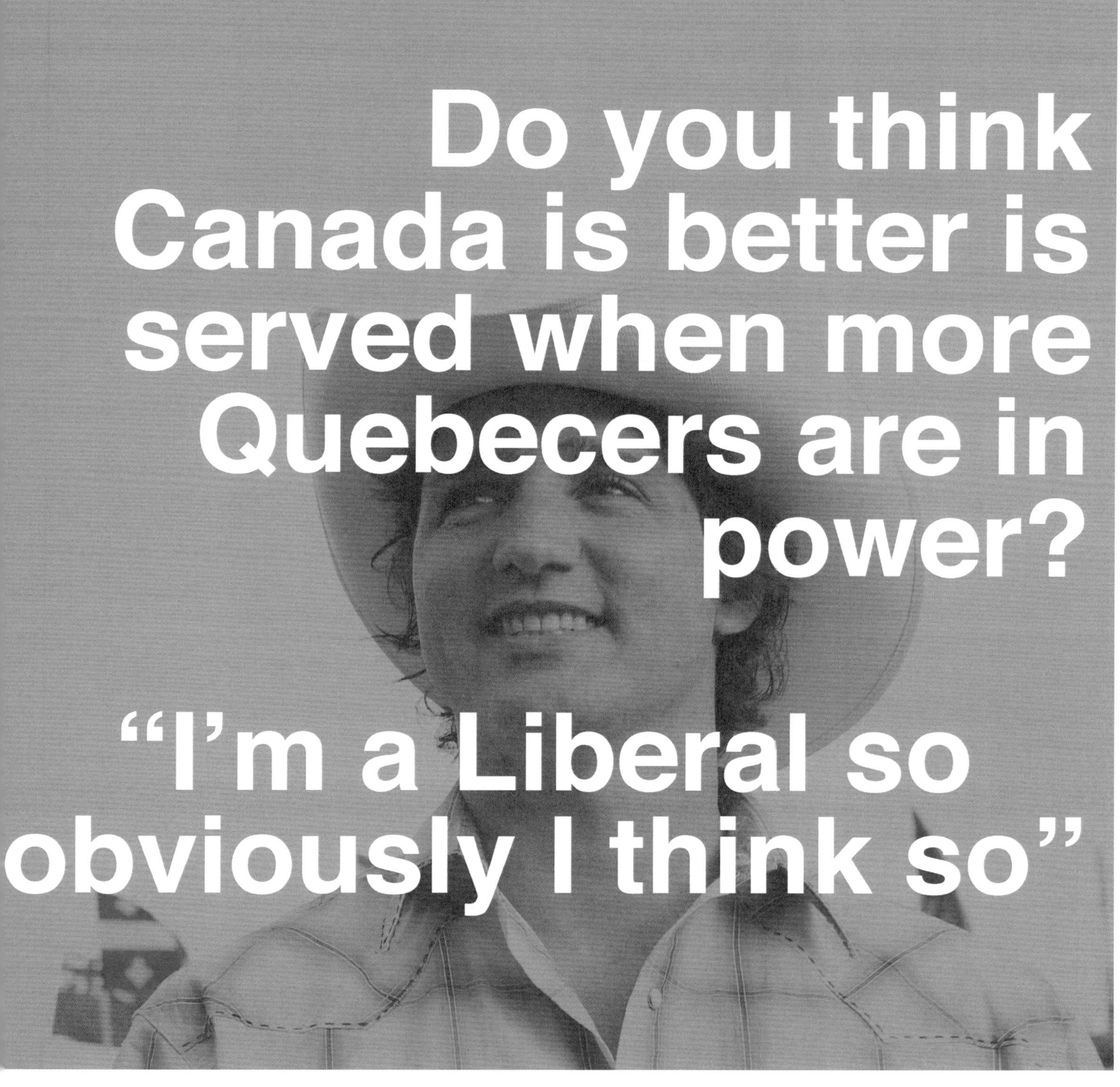

Do you think Canada is better is served when more Quebecers are in power?

"I'm a Liberal so obviously I think so"

Under PM Pierre Trudeau, Western Canadians felt their government didn't represent them. Pierre's policies were so disastrous for Western Canada, that they gave birth to a Western alienation movement.

Every leader since has been made to pay great attention to Western Canada's legitimate gripes about the federal government.

Prime Ministers Mulroney, Chrétien and Martin each made significant attempts to connect with Western Canadians and understand the unique issues they face.

With the election of Prime Minister Harper, it seemed that Canada had forever put Western discontent and alienation behind us.

Then, Justin Trudeau got elected.

For Saint Justin, Western Canadians – and particularly Albertans and their dirty oil – are nothing but an embarrassing blight on Confederation.

Trudeau mocks Albertans, he has open derision for the Western way of life, and, like father, like son, he is carelessly fanning the flame of Western alienation.

**Preston Manning:**
**"The West wants in!"**

**Stephen Harper:**
**"The West is in!"**

**Justin Trudeau:**
**"I want my Canada back!"**

# On Science

“We have to rethink elements as basic as space and time, to go all science fiction-y on you”

Former Liberal Leader Michael Ignatieff said of Justin Trudeau, “he’s an actor, a professional politician, (and he’s) always known that this was the role he was born to play.”

Understanding that Justin is an actor playing the role of Prime Minister, rather than actually being a Prime Minister, is a helpful thought experiment. It particularly helps understand why he is so good at duping the media into giving him glowing coverage.

During a staged media event at a quantum computing lab in Waterloo, Ontario, Trudeau asked reporters to ask him how quantum computing works. He had, after all, just toured the facility and spoken with some of Canada’s top physicists.

When journalists refused to indulge him – knowing full well he had probably memorized a Wikipedia entry on quantum computing – Trudeau ignored the question he had received and pretended he had been asked about computers.

Those not in the room fell into Trudeau’s trap, and praised him for being super smart on top of being super sexy!

And the academy award goes too…

**Reporter:**
**“When do you expect Canada’s ISIL mission to begin again and are we not doing anything in the interim while we prepare?”**

**Trudeau:**
**“Kay, very simply, normal computers work by” (laughter from the crowd) “no, no, no, don’t interrupt me. When you walk out of here, you will know more about quantum computing”**

# On Being a Hypocrite

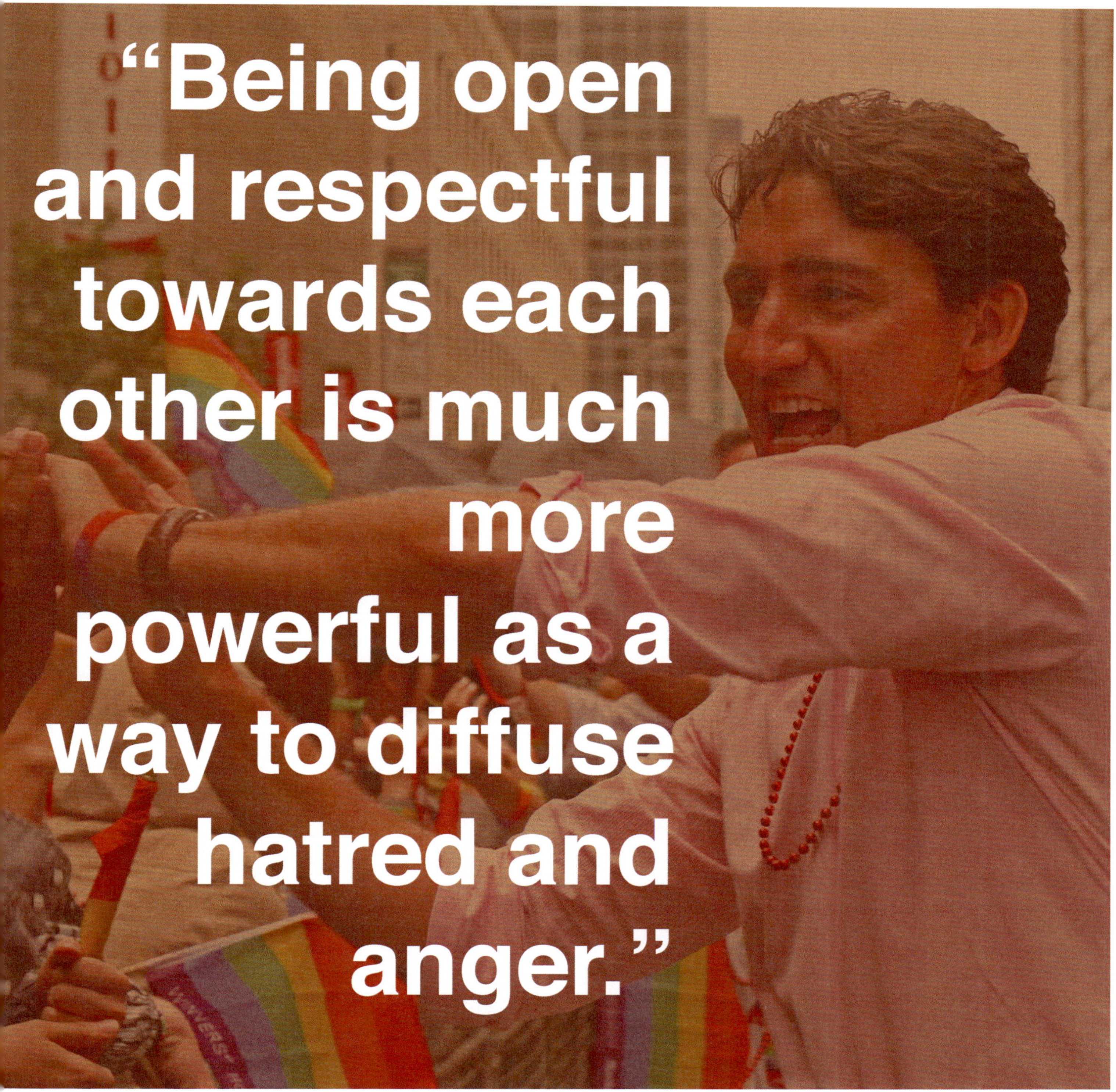

"Being open and respectful towards each other is much more powerful as a way to diffuse hatred and anger."

Justin Trudeau was elected by stealing a page from Barack Obama's playbook. He didn't just steal a page, he exported the entire campaign book and some of the campaign staff.

Hope is a powerful campaign slogan.

Unfortunately for voters, it's also empty rhetoric. By the end of Obama's 8 years in office, the majority of Americans believed that their country was headed in the wrong direction.

Trudeau, too, capitalized off of the desire for Hope and Change. He was at the right place at the right time. He was leader of the third party and was trailing in the polls throughout the campaign.

Suddenly, with just a few weeks left in the campaign, Trudeau's star began to rise, and, next thing we knew, he was Prime Minister.

Trudeau's hopeful optimism and boyish charm captured the imagination of Canadians. Well, of 39% of the electorate and 19% of the Canadian population who voted Liberal.

Turns out Trudeau's Mr. Nice guy routine doesn't apply when dealing with conservatives, and he certainly doesn't practice respect or manners in the House of Commons. Sorry!

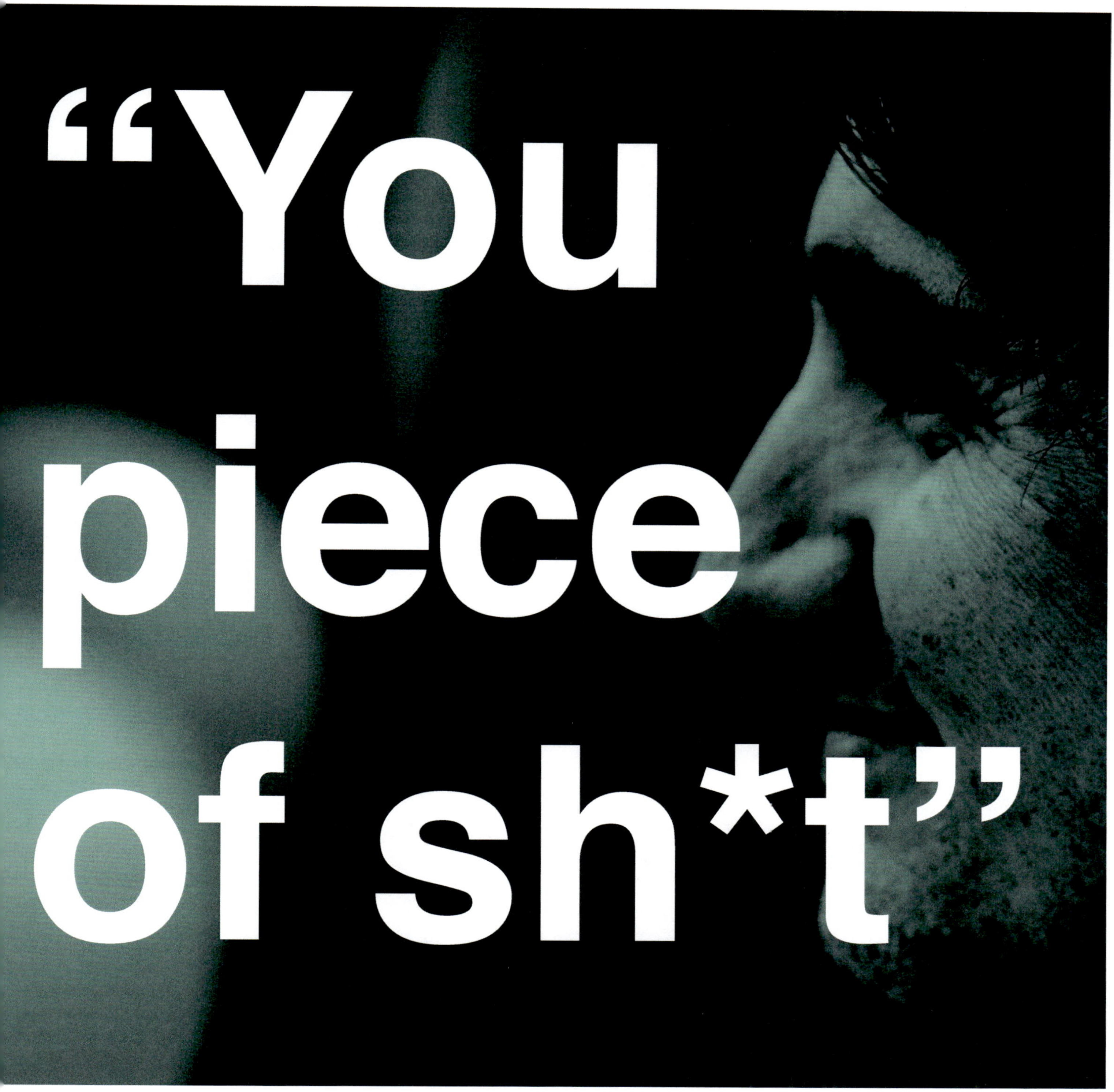

"You piece of sh*t"

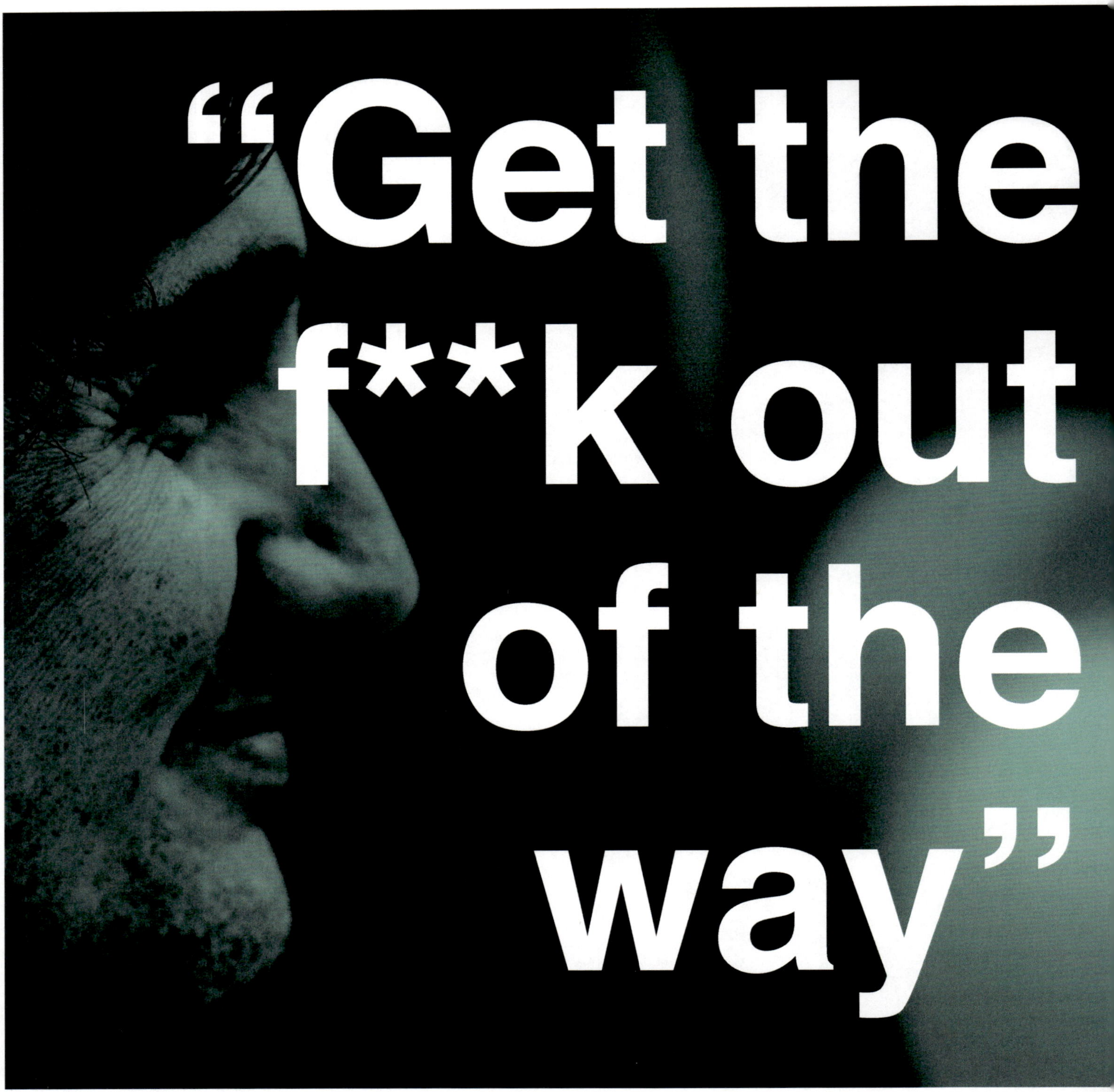

"Get the f**k out of the way"

In the House of Commons responding to a motion accusing him of "physical molestation" of a Member of Parliament:

"Mr. Speaker, I would like to take a moment to apologize... I should not have made physical contact with the member. I apologize... for my inappropriate contact"

“I have been, in the past, a very rare user of marijuana. I think 5 or 6 times in my life that I’ve taken a puff”

It came as no surprise to anyone when Justin Trudeau admitted that he smoked pot. The guy was a snow-bunny who spent his winters hanging out in Whistler, BC – marijuana capital of Canada and a mecca for potheads worldwide.

What makes Justin Trudeau a massive, insufferable hypocrite, though, is that he also admitted to smoking pot after being elected, as a sitting Member of Parliament.

Trudeau's blasé admission to smoking pot – a criminal offence in Canada – is an insult to both the police and his fellow pot-smokers who face criminal charges for smoking pot.

Trudeau ran on a platform of legalizing marijuana; his party proposes a state-takeover of the marijuana industry so it can be taxed, regulated and used to fill government coffers.

But when it came to decriminalizing pot in the meantime, Trudeau said in the House of Commons that he categorically opposes decriminalization. He stood in favour of slapping other pot users with criminal records - for a crime that won't be a crime if he ever gets around to implementing his pot promise.

Pot? Kettle. Black.

“My idea of freedom is that we should protect the rights of people to believe what their conscience dictates”

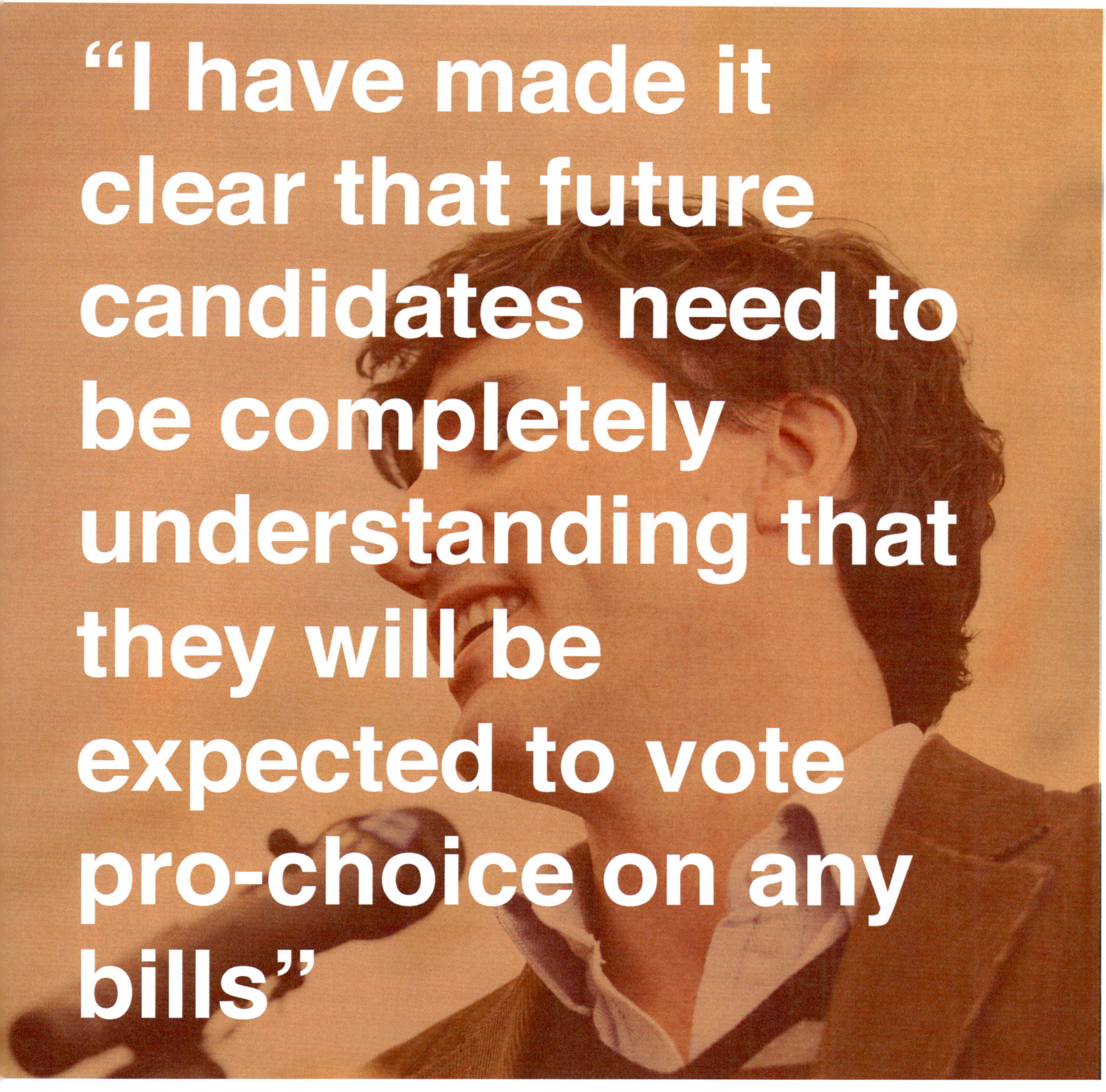

"I have made it clear that future candidates need to be completely understanding that they will be expected to vote pro-choice on any bills"

# On being Qualified to be Prime Minister

"I was a snowboard instructor, I was a bouncer in a nightclub, I was a whitewater river guide for many years. I worked as a teacher"

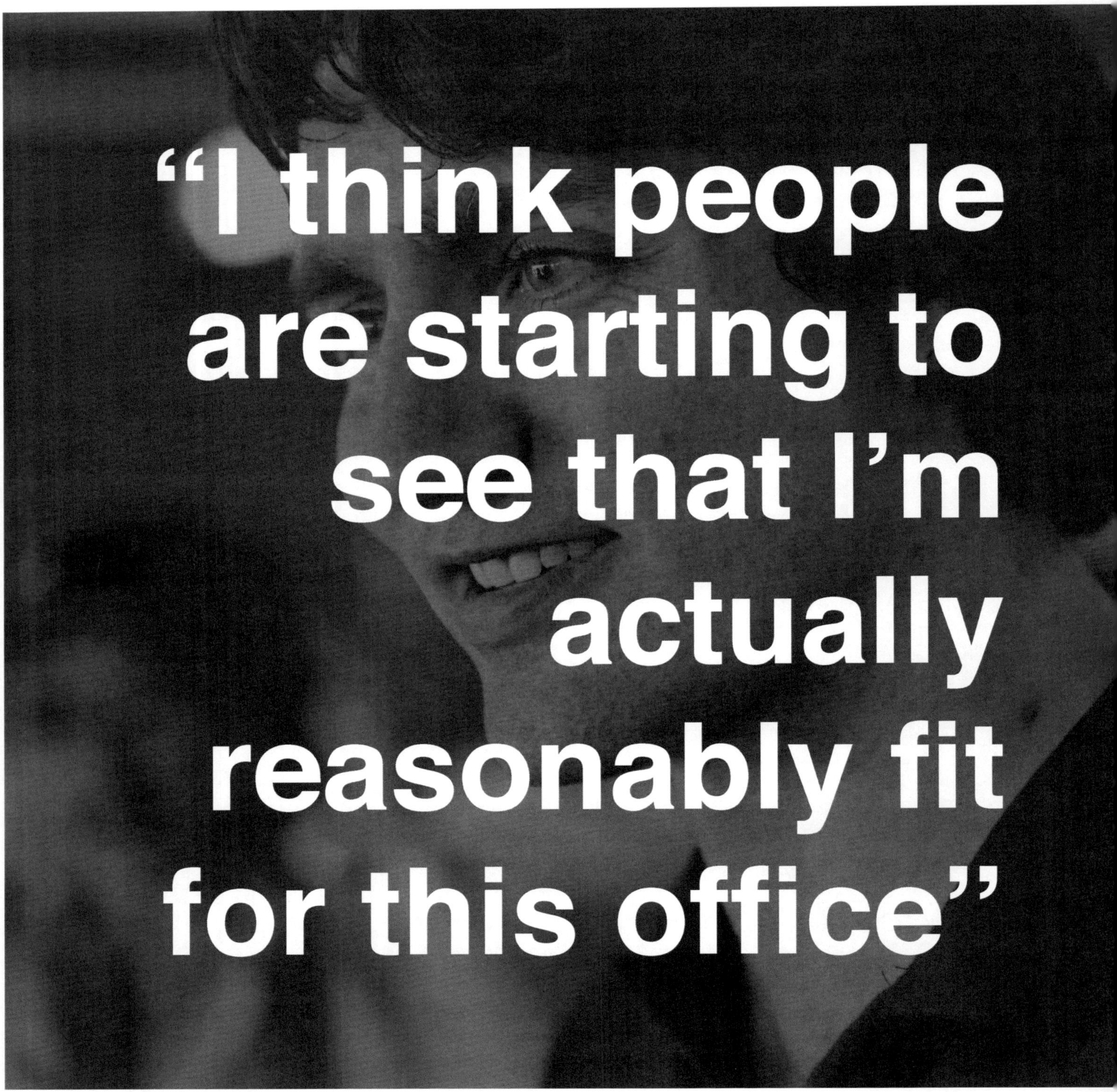

“I think people are starting to see that I’m actually reasonably fit for this office”

Trudeau's name and his father's legacy got him elected. But Trudeau junior certainly hasn't thought things through like his father.

Pierre Trudeau had an affinity for Mussolini and fascism as a young man, and a love for Cuba and China, two of the world's most repressive socialist regimes; but at least he was also a thoughtful and accomplished man.

He studied at Harvard, wrote long essays about public life in Canada, and gave considerable thought to the policies he championed. Pierre Trudeau was a scholar, an author, an activist and a visionary.

Justin Trudeau, by contrast, spent his twenties and thirties having a good ole time.

He travelled the world, smoked pot, enrolled and dropped out of several university degree programs and did odd jobs, including stints as a snowboarding instructor, night club bouncer, and actor. In his three-year teaching career, he taught junior school French and served as the back-up drama teacher.

That's not typically the path a politician takes to becoming Prime Minister. Luckily for Justin, his last name is Trudeau and he is really, really, really ridiculously good-looking.

# On his Governing Philosophy

# “Sunny ways, my friends, sunny ways”

Justin Trudeau won the birth lottery.  He was born in a famous political family, in the greatest country in the world. He inherited the prerequisite qualities for being Prime Minister, without ever having to do or accomplish anything.

Justin just needed to be Justin.

He was born on Christmas Day. And for the Liberal Party of Canada, who, in 2011 was decimated in their worst election loss in Canadian history, Justin Trudeau became their saviour.

But there has also been an unsettling aspect to his leadership. You never quite know what you're going to get. You're always left wondering, who is the man behind the selfies?

To quote Canadian legend and political commentator Rex Murphy, "does Trudeau earn all the attention-getting because he radiates inspired mature leadership, or because he is one of those "famous-for-being-famous" types?"

"Is the Trudeau phenomenon fandom or is it a wild response to genuine leadership?"

This book shows Justin Trudeau, in his own words. The raw, unedited version of Justin helps answer the question of whether Trudeau is a serious person, or whether he just plays one on TV.

# Photos Used Under Creative Commons License

| | | | |
|---|---|---|---|
| 1 | Justin Trudeau, Flickr | 21 | Mohammad Jangda, Flickr |
| 2 | Justin Trudeau, Flickr | 22 | Justin Trudeau, Flickr |
| 3 | Justin Trudeau, Flickr | 23 | Justin Trudeau, Flickr |
| 4 | Mohammad Jangda, Flickr | 24 | White House Website |
| 5 | Justin Trudeau, Flickr | 25 | Justin Trudeau, Flickr |
| 6 | Justin Trudeau, Flickr | 26 | Alex Guiord, Flickr |
| 7 | Norman Einstein, Wiki | 27 | Justin Trudeau, Flickr |
| 8 | Marcelo Montecino, Flickr | 28 | Justin Trudeau, Flickr |
| 9 | Justin Trudeau, Flickr | 29 | Justin Trudeau, Flickr |
| 10 | Justin Trudeau, Flickr | 30 | Justin Trudeau, Flickr |
| 11 | World Bank, Flickr | 31 | Joseph Morris, Flickr |
| 12 | White House Website | 32 | Alex Guiord, Flickr |
| 13 | US Army, Wiki | 33 | Justin Trudeau, Flickr |
| 14 | Justin Trudeau, Flickr | 34 | Justin Trudeau, Flickr |
| 15 | Carlos Menendez, Flickr | 35 | Charles Barilleaux, Flickr |
| 16 | Justin Trudeau, Flickr | 36 | Justin Trudeau, Flickr |
| 17 | Paul Evert, Flickr | 37 | Justin Trudeau, Flickr |
| 18 | Justin Trudeau, Flickr | 38 | Gov Alberta, Flickr |
| 19 | Justin Trudeau, Flickr | 39 | Justin Trudeau, Flickr |
| 20 | Justin Trudeau, Flickr | 0 | Taha Ghaznavi, Flickr |

## About Candice Malcolm

Candice Malcolm is a nationally-syndicated columnist with the Toronto Sun, a senior fellow with the True North Initiative, a fellow with the Canadian Global Affairs Institute and an international fellow with the Centre for a Secure Free Society in Washington, D.C. She is a former advisor to the Minister of Citizenship and Immigration Canada, the former director of research at Sun News Network, and from 2012 to 2014, she served as the Ontario Director of the Canadian Taxpayer's Federation.

Candice is the author of two best-selling books, Generation Screwed and Losing True North.

Born and raised in Vancouver, British Columbia, Candice is a ninth generation Canadian and loves to travel. She has master's degrees in international relations and international law, and splits her time between Toronto and San Francisco with her husband Kasra.

Source for all quotes at
www.candicemalcolm.com/stupidthings